COWARD

D1242108

in an hour

BY HOWARD KISSEL

SUSAN C. MOORE, SERIES EDITOR

PLAYWRIGHTS in an hour

know the playwright, love the play

IN AN HOUR BOOKS • HANOVER, NEW HAMPSHIRE • INANHOURBOOKS.COM
AN IMPRINT OF SMITH AND KRAUS PUBLISHERS, INC • SMITHANDKRAUS.COM

With grateful thanks to Carl R. Mueller, whose fascinating introductions to his translations of the Greek and German playwrights provided inspiration for this series.

Published by In an Hour Books
an imprint of Smith and Kraus, Inc.
177 Lyme Road, Hanover, NH 03755
inanhourbooks.com SmithandKraus.com

Know the playwright, love the play.

In an Hour, In a Minute, and Theater IQ are registered trademarks of
In an Hour Books.

Front cover design by Dan Mehling, dmehling@gmail.com
Text design by Kate Mueller, Electric Dragon Productions
Book production by Dede Cummings Design, DCDesign@sover.net

ISBN-13: 978-1-936232-10-9
ISBN-10: 1-936232-10-3
Library of Congress Control Number: 2009943212

CONTENTS

Why Playwrights in an Hour?

This new series by Smith and Kraus Publishers titled Playwrights in an Hour has a dual purpose for being: one academic, the other general. For the general reader, this volume, as well as the many others in the series, offers in compact form the information needed for a basic understanding and appreciation of the works of each volume's featured playwright. Which is not to say that there don't exist volumes on end devoted to each playwright under consideration. But inasmuch as few are blessed with enough time to read the splendid scholarship that is available, a brief, highly focused accounting of the playwright's life and work is in order. The central feature of the series, a thirty- to forty-page essay, integrates the playwright into the context of his or her time and place. The volumes, though written to high standards of academic integrity, are accessible in style and approach to the general reader as well as to the student and, of course, to the theater professional and theatergoer. These books will serve for the brushing up of one's knowledge of a playwright's career, to the benefit of theater work or theatergoing. The Playwrights in an Hour series represents all periods of Western theater: Aeschylus to Shakespeare to Wedekind to Ibsen to Williams to Beckett, and on to the great contemporary playwrights who continue to offer joy and enlightenment to a grateful world.

Carl R. Mueller
School of Theater, Film and Television
Department of Theater
University of California, Los Angeles

Introduction

In many ways, Noël Coward is a unique British playwright. But he also belongs to a long tradition of English wit dramatists (many of them Anglo-Irish), who have been amusing audiences with acerbic love tourneys ever since Shakespeare first had Beatrice joust with Benedict in *Much Ado About Nothing*. This tradition was to flower again after the Restoration under such seventeenth-century masters of the genre as John Dryden, George Etherege, William Wycherly, and, preeminently, William Congreve. It was to continue into the eighteenth century in the plays of Oliver Goldsmith and Richard Brinsley Sheridan. And it would experience another brilliant flowering in the nineteenth and twentieth centuries in the works of Oscar Wilde, Bernard Shaw, and Noël Coward.

More than that of any other country, the drama of Great Britain has been celebrated for its verbal dexterity. But what constitutes wit in one age can be a very different element in another. Perhaps some clever graduate student will some day help us understand the seismic shift in style between the sensual, vitalist language of, say, Shakespeare's Sir John Falstaff in the Elizabethan period ("not only witty in myself, but the cause that wit is in other men") and the more effete wordplay of Etherege's Sir Foppington Flutter in the Restoration age. Whatever the case, it is not the corpulent Falstaff of *Henry IV* but the more elegant poseur in *The Man of Mode* who exercises the most lasting influence on future British dramatists, including Noël Coward.

Coward, by his own admission, was always a bit more of a lightweight than his witty predecessors. Nonetheless, he had a talent for slashing the verbal saber and wielding the repartee épée. Oscar Wilde had said that the secret of art was treating trivial things humorously and humorous things trivially. Coward took that epigram to heart. Still, unlike Wilde in his plays, Noël Coward did not always send off comic sparks. And while Wilde considered patriotism to be "the virtue of the vicious,"

Coward was not at all reluctant to express patriotic sentiments (as in the film *In Which We Serve*). Nor did he shy away from romantic ones (as in the short play *Still Life* on which the film *Brief Encounter* was based). For all his wit, Coward was essentially a Romantic, and he continues to live not only in such sophisticated offerings as *Private Lives* and *Design for Living*, but also in his repertory of sentimental songs like "I'll See You Again" and "Somewhere I'll Find You."

Coward was not just a playwright and composer, he was also a performer, and the character he developed — suave, soigné, elegant, and remote — was to become a crucial persona of English culture, almost defining for a while the nature of the English aristocracy. The Angry Young Men, among them John Osborne and Harold Pinter, thought they were rebelling against Coward, a bastion of the elite establishment — and for a while Coward thought so, too. But the fact is that Osborne's dialogue, for example in *Look Back in Anger*, like Pinter's in *Betrayal*, would have been impossible without the witty banter of Noël Coward. He was, and continues to remain, the most powerful stylistic influence on modern British drama.

Robert Brustein
Founding Director of the Yale and American Repertory Theatres
Distinguished Scholar in Residence, Suffolk University
Senior Research Fellow, Harvard University

Coward

IN A MINUTE

AGE	DATE	
—	**1899**	**Enter Noël Coward.**
6	1905	Oscar Wilde — *De Profundis,* published posthumously
8	1907	Pablo Picasso — *Les Desmoiselles d'Avignon*
13	1912	The Oreo cookie debuts in Chelsea, New York.
17	1916	James Joyce — *Portrait of an Artist as a Young Man*
19	**1918**	**Noël Coward — *The Rat Trap***
20	1919	George Bernard Shaw — *Heartbreak House*
23	1922	The Irish Free State is formed as a self-governing dominion of Britain.
27	**1926**	**Noël Coward — *This Was a Man***
30	1929	Vatican City is born as an independent state.
31	**1930**	**Noël Coward — *Private Lives***
32	1931	Al Capone is sentenced to eleven years in prison for tax evasion.
33	1932	Betty Boop plays the lead role in *Stopping the Show*
34	1933	Bertolt Brecht — *The Seven Deadly Sins*
37	1936	Anastasio Somoza Garcia seizes power in Nicaragua.
39	1938	Britain signs Munich pact with Hitler; Chamberlain announces "Peace for our time."
40	1939	The New York World's Fair opens.
41	1940	Bacon, butter, ham, eggs, and sugar are rationed in Britain.
42	**1941**	**Noël Coward — *Blithe Spirit***
46	1945	Percy Spencer patents microwave oven.
48	**1947**	**Noël Coward — *Peace in our Time* performed in London**
51	1950	U.S. President Harry Truman orders development of the hydrogen bomb.
52	**1951**	**Noël Coward — *Relative Values***
54	1953	Edmund Hillary and Tenzing Norgay conquer Mount Everest.
59	1958	Harold Pinter — *The Birthday Party*
60	1959	Watson and Crick discover the double-helix structure of DNA.
63	1962	Cuban missile crisis brings the U.S. and the U.S.S.R to the brink of nuclear war.
68	**1967**	**Noël Coward — *Star Quality***
70	1969	Neil Armstrong takes "one small step" on the moon with Apollo 11 mission.
74	**1973**	**Exit Noël Coward.**

A snapshot of the playwright's world. From historical events to pop-culture and the literary landscape of the time, this brief list catalogues events that directly or indirectly impacted the playwright's writing. Play citations refer to premiere dates.

Coward

DRAMA

The Rat Trap

I'll Leave It to You

Sirocco

The Young Idea

London Calling!

The Queen Was in the Parlour

The Vortex

On with the Dance

Fallen Angels

Hay Fever

Easy Virtue

This Was a Man

Semi-Monde

Home Chat

The Marquise

This Year of Grace

Bitter Sweet

Private Lives

Post-Mortem

Cavalcade

Words and Music

Design for Living

Conversation Piece

Point Valaine

Tonight at 8:30 (nine one-acts)

Operette

This section presents a complete list of the playwright's works in chronological order.

AUTOBIOGRAPHY

DIARIES

NOVEL

SHORT STORIES

To Step Aside
Star Quality
Collected Short Stories
Pretty Polly Barlow, and Other Stories
Bon Voyage, and Other Stories

VERSE

The Noël Coward Song Book
The Lyrics of Noël Coward
Not Yet the Dodo
Collected Verse

SATIRE

A Withered Nosegay
Chelsea Buns
Spangled Unicorn
Terribly Intimate Portraits

SCREENPLAYS

In Which We Serve
Brief Encounter

Onstage with Coward

Introducing Colleagues and Contemporaries
of Noël Coward

 THEATER
Samuel Beckett, Irish playwright
Bertolt Brecht, German playwright
Lynn Fontanne, English actress
Gertrude Lawrence, English actress
Alfred Lunt, American actor
Arthur Miller, American playwright
Terrence Rattigan, English playwright
Thornton Wilder, American playwright

 ARTS
Ansel Adams, American photographer
Marcel Duchamp, French artist
Duke Ellington, American composer and musician
Ella Fitzgerald, American musician
Lorenz Hart, American lyricist
Cole Porter, American lyricist
Pablo Picasso, Spanish artist
Vaughn Williams, English composer

 FILM
Ingrid Bergman, Swedish actress
Humphrey Bogart, American actor
Charlie Chaplin, English actor and director
Federico Fellini, Italian director
Katharine Hepburn, American actress

This section lists contemporaries whom the playwright may or may not have known.

Alfred Hitchcock, English director
Laurence Olivier, English actor and director
Orson Welles, American director

POLITICS/MILITARY

Winston Churchill, British prime minister
Elizabeth II, queen of England
Dwight D. Eisenhower, American president and general
Charles de Gaulle, French president
Adolf Hitler, German dictator
Benito Mussolini, Italian dictator
Harold Wilson, British prime minister
Woodrow Wilson, American president

SCIENCE

Jacques-Yves Cousteau, French marine explorer
Francis Crick, English molecular biologist
Marie Curie, Russian-French physicist and chemist
Albert Einstein, German physicist
Alexander Fleming, Scottish biologist and pharmacologist
Jonas Salk, American research scientist
James Watson, American molecular biologist
Edwin Hubble, American astronomer

LITERATURE

F. Scott Fitzgerald, American novelist
Ernest Hemingway, American novelist
Aldous Huxley, English writer
W. Somerset Maugham, English novelist
Vladimir Nabokov, Russian novelist
George Orwell, English novelist and journalist
Evelyn Waugh, English wit and novelist
Virginia Woolf, English novelist and essayist

RELIGION/PHILOSOPHY

Dalai Lama, Tibetan religious and political leader
Mohandas K. Gandhi, Indian political and spiritual leader
Billy Graham, American evangelical religious leader
Martin Luther King Jr., American activist and clergyman
Malcolm X, American activist and Muslim leader
Ayn Rand, Russian-American philosopher
Jean-Paul Sartre, French philosopher
Mother Teresa, Albanian nun

SPORTS

Roger Bannister, English runner
René Lacoste, French tennis player
Joe Louis, American boxer
Helen Wills Moody, American tennis player
Jesse Owens, American track and field athlete
Satchel Paige, American baseball player
Jackie Robinson, American baseball player
Gene Sarazen, American golfer

INDUSTRY/BUSINESS

Walt and Roy Disney, American founders of Walt Disney
     Productions
Henry Ford, American industrialist
William Fox, American founder of Fox Film Corporation
Howard Hughes, American industrialist and film producer
William Randolph Hearst, American newspaper magnate
Masaru Ibuka, Japanese founder of Sony
Samuel Walton, American founder of Walmart
Adolph Zukor, Hungarian film mogul

COWARD

in an hour

"MAD DOGS" AND WORLD AFFAIRS

In August 1941, two great ships, one British, the other American, converged in Placentia Bay, off the coast of Newfoundland. Britain was already at war with Nazi Germany. In a few months, America would be also. The war would be governed by the decisions made by the two powerful men the ships had clandestinely borne to this remote destination.

The two men had met in 1918, when the American, an assistant secretary of the navy, had been part of a delegation to London that the Englishman, then the minister of munitions, had briefed on modern weaponry. In October 1933, the Englishman, now far from the corridors of power, had sent an inscribed copy of the first volume of his biography of his ancestor, the Duke of Marlborough, to the American, who had been elected president of the United States.

This was, however, the first time Winston Churchill and Franklin Delano Roosevelt met as prime minister and president. By all accounts, they got on famously.

This is the core of the book. The essay places the playwright in the context of his or her world and analyzes the influences and inspirations within that world.

The only major disagreement between them during the conference — and it was apparently quite heated — was over the lyrics to Noël Coward's "Mad Dogs and Englishmen" They argued over whether the line "In Bangkok at 12 o'clock they foam at the mouth and run" came at the end of the first or second refrain.

Coward claimed he wrote the song in his head — "without paper, pen or piano" — while traveling from Hanoi to Saigon in 1930. Its first public performance came in a revue two years later, and it instantly became iconic. Not only did the president of the United States know it by heart, but he apparently knew it better than the prime minister of England. It was Roosevelt who won the argument in Newfoundland.

On the one hand, the witty song seems a quintessential expression of elitist England, the England where everyone — everyone being the population residing in Mayfair — dresses for dinner. But on the other, the song was embraced by a population far greater than Mayfair because it paradoxically came to represent England itself — starchy, prim but valiant, and tenacious. It is both self-satiric and deeply self-celebratory.

Churchill had asked Coward to contribute to the war effort, and Coward was excited by the prospect of doing intelligence work (which he did very briefly, in Paris, until the arrival of the Nazis). No, Churchill said. He wanted him to sing "Mad Dogs and Englishmen" to entertain the troops. Coward balked, thinking soldiers would be put off by it. Again, the paradox is that the troops, few of whom would have felt at home in Mayfair, adored the song — and its creator.

A LIFE OF PARADOX

As we survey the life and work of Noël Coward, this paradox is always present. On the one hand, he represents the snobbish world of the English drawing room. Many of the roles Coward wrote for himself required him to wear luxurious dressing gowns and wield long cigarette holders. Coward was friendly with the Bright Young Things who sought to subvert the Victorian values of their parents, dressing gowns and all. With no pretense of being an agitator, he brought their concerns to the stage.

Moreover, he also understood the England of fish 'n' chips and the music hall. What tribute to the English spirit remains as moving as his film *In Which We Serve*? Or the song he wrote surveying his native city on a morning after a particularly brutal German bombing, "London Pride"?

From a very early age, Noël Coward was not just a wildly successful actor and playwright but also a public figure. Few men of the theater in any age have had as large and diverse an audience as Coward did — in large part because much of his theatrical output was musical. His music, which often bordered on the sentimental but was equally often witty and full of melancholy, appealed to an audience that might never have seen his plays. (Even "Mad Dogs" found an unlikely interpreter in Joe Cocker in 1970. Cocker's audience hardly fell within the range of what anyone might consider Coward admirers.)

For his contemporaries, Noël Coward was considered The Master, a title that began early in his career as ironic but quickly became incontestable.

EARLY YEARS

His gifts manifested themselves quite early. He was born on December 16, 1899, in Teddington-on-Thames, a genteel suburb southwest of London. His name came from his birthday's proximity to Christmas, and it was a source of annoyance that, unlike other children, who received presents for both their birthday and the holiday, he had to make do with a single gift for both.

His father Arthur's family was musical. He was a not very successful piano salesman. Many of his relatives sang in church choirs. It was his mother, Violet, who was the theater lover.

She saw everything she could by the two great idols of late Victorian England, Sir Henry Irving and Ellen Terry (she kept the programs, as well as many years of correspondence with her increasingly famous son, until she died). A stage mother when the term itself was in its infancy, she took her son to his first play, a pantomime called *Aladdin*, when he was only four.

She also took him to musical comedies as a very young child. At the turn-of-the-century, English musical comedies were much like operettas, such as *The Waltz Dream* and *The Chocolate Soldier* — which may be why much of Coward's music, especially for his best-known operetta, *Bitter Sweet*, has an operetta-like quality.

In January 1911, shortly after Coward had turned eleven, through his mother's determined efforts, he appeared in an amateur production called *The Goldfish* in the role of Prince Mussel. His performance was singled out by a newspaper reviewer. That fall he was engaged by Sir Charles Hawtrey, a successful actor-manager, to play a pageboy in *The Great Name*. His professional career had begun.

He appeared in the West End, the commercial center of British theater shortly thereafter and toured the provinces for much of his childhood. In 1913, he played Slightly, one of the Lost Boys in Sir James Barrie's *Peter Pan*, in the annual production of the play during the holidays in London. Where other children his age were encountering adolescence, the teenaged Coward was being grounded in theater, particularly the light theater that was popular fare in England even during World War I. He made his first appearance in a musical in 1916.

If his professional life familiarized him with the conventions of the theater, he was also quickly becoming acquainted with the ways of the world. When he was fourteen, he became the close friend (some have conjectured the lover) of a society painter named Philip Streatfield, who was more than twice his age. A year later, Streatfield died of tuberculosis, but his society friends continued to look after young Coward.

EARLY STAGES

As a result, by the time he wrote his first play, he was not only an extremely experienced theater artist but an observer at very close range of the high life that was the staple of West End theater.

The most august figure of the London stage in the '20s, when Coward began to write, was Bernard Shaw, who would win the Nobel Prize in 1925. Much of Shaw's early output was devoted to satirizing the conventions of the well-made plays of the late nineteenth century. It should be remembered that he did not have his first commercial success until 1911 with *Fanny's First Play*, in which he lampooned his fellow theater critics. His first truly popular play, *Pygmalion*, came two years later, when he was three years short of sixty.

By contrast, Coward, a very young man, had no interest in questioning the assumptions of the commercial theater. Unlike Shaw, who had spent many years as a critic and socialist provocateur, Coward brought no philosophical baggage to the stage. It was simply where he chose to make his living.

One of the things that made the stage different for Coward was that he wrote after the harrowing experience of World War I. The late Victorian and Edwardian eras in which Shaw wrote were periods when a social critic could challenge certainties.

That was not the case after the tectonic shifts of World War I. There was an ironic undertow to the phrase *Bright Young Things*, which characterized the youth of the '20s. Yes, they had wealth, good looks, and social ease. But many of their closest friends had died on the battlefields of France or come home shell-shocked. Certainty was no longer an option.

Even the class system, against which Brits continue to rail, though it held sway, was suddenly vulnerable. The theatricality of Coward's plays reflects a sense that identity, especially identity as governed by class, was no longer something one had to accept.

If his plays have an improvisational quality, it is perhaps because for the first time, probably since the late eighteenth century — when the notion of class came to be increasingly fixed — one could create oneself, especially in the world of the theater. Coward may have been his own greatest creation, but his characters share his eagerness to present themselves as if upon a stage.

Many of Coward's major characters are inordinately charming — as they would need to be in seeking the favor of the people around them, who may or may not be delighted by the idea of existing as an audience.

Coward's first play, *I'll Leave It to You*, was produced in the West End in 1920, when he was twenty. The reviews were mixed but largely favorable. The play ran for only a month, and although Coward continued to write, he supported himself as an actor.

EARLY SUCCESS

He scored his first great success as a writer four years later with *The Vortex*. In retrospect, it seems amazing that a play with its themes should have been permitted on the London stage, whose content was rigidly controlled until the late 1960s by an official censor, the Lord Chamberlain. Coward had to make a personal case for the play to the Lord Chamberlain, who, understandably, considered it "unpleasant."

As late as the morning of the premiere, it was not certain permission would be granted. Happily, it was. Coward had persuaded the Lord Chamberlain that the play, which was in fact quite raw, was a moral tract. The argument is plausible, though that is probably not how most audiences experience the play.

The premiere took place in a little theater in Hampstead, then a suburb north of London, very much the equivalent of Off Broadway. The first night audience, however, was by no means a Bohemian lot. In it were Coward's friends from the highest reaches of society, including Lady Louis Mountbatten. The opening night caused a sensation, and West End managers vied to present it in a commercial production.

The Vortex had its genesis in an incident involving Coward's close friend, Stewart Forster, who was an officer in the Coldstream Guards. Forster had invited him to dinner in a London club. When their party entered, one of the girls in it pointed to an older woman across the room carrying on with a man half her age. She called her a "hag." Coward was appalled. The woman was Forster's mother. He immediately went to her side and made a great show of gallantry toward her.

Coward realized the theatrical value of a woman who had younger lovers. He also wanted to create a juicy part for himself and knew that he was unsuited to playing a dashing officer. The play he created did not display the same courtesy toward the older woman that Coward did toward his friend's mother. Nor did he give himself the sort of brittle young playboy he could easily have played. He made the character the son of a drug addict.

For many, the high point of *The Vortex* was a speech Nicky, the son — the role Coward played — delivers to his mother late in the play. He berates her for chasing after one of his friends, that is to say, a man half her age. Shortly afterward, he reveals his drug habit to her and begs her finally to act as a real mother toward him. It is a shattering conclusion to a play that begins in what one might regard as typical Noël Coward banter.

With *The Vortex*, Coward made himself a force in the West End. Within two years, he had written several other plays whose theatrical viability remains undiminished eighty years later.

One of them was *Fallen Angels*, which featured a drunk scene between two women that made it a scandalous success. The two actresses in the original production were Edna Best and Tallulah Bankhead. The prudishness of the reviewers in their denunciations of *Fallen Angels* helped enormously at the box office. So did the stars.

Coward achieved a trifecta in this two-year time frame with the 1925 *Hay Fever*, which he actually wrote several years earlier. In 1921, when his career in London had yet to ignite, Coward decided to go to

New York. He went virtually on the spur of the moment because a close friend, Jeffery Amherst, yet another handsome officer in the Coldstream Guards, was sailing there and invited Coward to join him. Coward agreed, though he had little money and not enough of a reputation to mean anything in New York.

ALFRED, LYNN, AND LAURETTE

The visit, however, had huge consequences. During his time there he befriended Alfred Lunt and Lynn Fontanne, who remained his friends and collaborators throughout their lives.

He also made the acquaintance of an actress who was then a great star because of her performance in a play called *Peg o' My Heart*, which captivated audiences in both New York and London before World War I. Her reputation today is based on something far more significant — originating the role of Amanda Wingfield in Tennessee Williams' *The Glass Menagerie*.

But that was decades in the future. In the '20s Taylor, who would go through severe alcoholism, still traded on her enormous success in *Peg o' My Heart.* She and her husband, the playwright Hartley Manners, had a grand house on Riverside Drive, where they entertained theater folk every Sunday evening. Coward quickly became a favorite of both of them.

One of the features of these lively parties was something called The Adverb Game, a kind of charadelike exercise in which a guest had to demonstrate performing some task in a way that the guests would understand the adverb that governed his action. It required great cleverness, skill, and courage — since the other guests were among the most talented actors in the New York theater. The most frightful part of the "audience" was Laurette Taylor herself, whose comments were likely to be acid.

GET THE GUESTS

Coward later wrote that he was surprised no one had seen what a great device The Adverb Game would be on the stage. He wrote a play shortly after he got back to London with a grande dame in the manner of Taylor whose country house is filled with guests invited by members of her family.

The guests, encouraged by the family to play games, endure great humiliation — a possible title for the play might have been "Get the Guests." Instead, Coward titled his finished work *Hay Fever*. Many years later, Edward Albee acknowledged this play as an inspiration for *Who's Afraid of Virginia Woolf?*

Coward showed it to one of the leading actresses of the London stage, Marie Tempest, shortly after he wrote it. She was not taken with it. But after the success of *The Vortex*, she thought better of it and asked to look at it again. This time she not only wanted to star in it but wanted the author to direct her.

Although the role she played, Judith, the matriarch of an eccentric, ultimately selfish, inconsiderate family, was clearly the starring part, one might say — especially for those early audiences — the star was Coward's dazzling use of the language. One might say *Hay Fever* was a play about nothing. As we know from the television show *Seinfeld* self-avowedly about nothing, what makes such an effort successful is the skill of the acting.

Hay Fever became a runaway sensation. Three hits in the West End consolidated Coward's reputation as the Man of the Hour.

SING A SCALE FOR ME

What may have been more important in building his audience was the many songs he wrote for musical revues, beginning with *London Calling!* in 1923. This revue was the first show in which Coward saw his name in lights, but in those days, the authorship of musical shows was secondary. He was one of several people who wrote the book, and he composed and performed many of the songs. He did not make an instantly positive impression. "He cannot compose," one of the critics declared. "And he should sing only for his friends' amazement."

Some of his lyrics are conventional. But others, such as in "What Love Means to Girls Like Me," apart from their clever rhymes, make adroit use of alliteration. One would not imagine this was the work of a novice.

In 1965, when Coward published a volume of his lyrics, he remembered a few lines he wrote as a child already mesmerized by the magic of rhyme. One rhyme remains impressive, and even if one didn't know the author, one might guess it:

> In a Voice of Soft Staccato
> We Will Speak of the Tomato.

The other he includes only because it is all he can remember of his early output, but he criticizes it justly simply by spelling it in the way he expected the speaker to mangle the natural rhythms:

> The Sinful AspaRAGus
> To Iniquity Will Drag Us.

One of the songs in *London Calling!*, "Parisian Pierrot," sets the tone for much of what he would write in the ensuing decade. This song is so much a Noël Coward staple — it remains one of his top ten songs — that it is easy to lose sight of how remarkable it was in the context of its time. As a newcomer, no one expected Coward to use the medium of the revue to write social commentary. Revues were supposed to be lighthearted, gay, romantic. By contrast, the lyrics for "Parisian Pierrot" are melancholy, understandably, since the inspiration was an image that haunted him — a puppet hanging in a shop window in Berlin. More important, the level of literacy is well above moon and June rhymes, though those were perfectly acceptable in the mid-1920s. The lyrics present a hardheaded look at a social phenomenon — the Bright Young

Thing whose exterior glamour masks a profound lack of ease. That this should have been part of a show intended to do no more than delight speaks well for the flexibility of the producers. It is, of course, important that the melody is also smooth and worldly.

Strangely, though his gift for melody was sublime, Coward had no musical training. He could pick out his tunes on the piano but could neither write them down nor harmonize them. Starting with *London Calling!*, these tasks were performed by a woman named Elsie April, to whom Coward was effusive in his public praise.

Just as there were unfounded rumors that Irving Berlin's music was really written by "a little colored boy," in the slang of the time, it was often thought that April was the true source of his melodies. But April was forthright about her inability to compose. During *Bitter Sweet*, when huge demands were being placed on Coward, he asked her to write a sixteen-bar transition for a piece. She simply could not.

The number was sung to great effect by Gertrude Lawrence. Cecil Beaton said she made it "the signature tune of the late '20s." Coward had met her more than a decade earlier when they were both preadolescent actors touring the provinces. It was a friendship and collaboration that would last all their lives.

Coward himself could be prickly, and certainly the world of the theater was not one known for its warmth. But it seems worth noting that throughout his career he remained deeply loyal to his friends. He had a great capacity for friendship. Working in the theater often tested these friendships, but in large part because of his keen understanding of people, the friendships survived the battles.

Although much of Coward's life fits brittle backstage stereotypes, Sir Tyrone Guthrie made the following observation in his memoir *A Life in the Theatre*.

> In *Hay Fever* one catches, between the lines, a glimpse of that aspect of Noel Coward which made him a good president of the Actors' Orphanage. Usually this position had gone to an

eminent actor who made a dignified figurehead, gave a hand-some subscription and saw to it that seven or eight of his well-off friends did the same. Coward did all this, but he also visited the orphanage, made sure that the beds were clean, that the slops were emptied, the stairs swept, the meals adequate and that the orphans felt that their president really stood in loco parentis.

During *London Calling!*, Coward established another collaboration with the great couturier Edward Molyneux, the British-born dress-maker who had the audacity — and talent — to establish his fashion headquarters on the Rue Royale in Paris. Molyneux, whose clients included Greta Garbo, Vivien Leigh, and Gertrude Lawrence, as well as some of the most fashionable ladies in London and members of the nobility, designed costumes for Coward's shows for many decades. He provided the visual scintillation to match Coward's words. Two years later in the 1925 *On with the Dance*, Coward wrote another archetypal lyric and correspondingly elegiac melody, "Poor Little Rich Girl."

At the end of the 1920s, Coward wrote something unexpected for someone with his very modern, ironic sensibility — an operetta, inspired while visiting friends in the country. His hostess put a recording of *Die Fledermaus* on her gramophone, and Coward found himself intoxicated by the idea of writing an operetta.

The result was *Bitter Sweet*, the title supplied by Alfred Lunt. It begins the year it was produced, 1929, in a grand house in Grosvenor Square. Lady Shayne, an older woman known to have led a Bohemian life in her youth, chastises the young people at the party she is giving. She tells them they know nothing beyond "noise and speed," and then sings "The Call of Life," in which she urges them to find love.

We then go back fifty years to see Lady Shayne as a young Englishwoman studying with a Viennese composer who is in love with her. She is about to return to England to be married. At their last lesson, her teacher gives her a song he wrote many years earlier, "I'll See You Again," which, he insists, he wrote with her in mind. The two are separated, then she returns to him. Back in Vienna, the young composer is killed in a duel. (With another act to go, the death of the romantic hero is hardly a commonplace of operetta.)

Happily on her return to London, she meets an older nobleman who marries her. Her early wild youth and misfortune are what entitle her to lecture the young people of the late '20s on their obligations to live life fully.

To modern eyes, much of the plot seems like pure operetta. But when the script was published in 1929, W. Somerset Maugham, one of the leading novelists of the day, made, in his introduction to the operetta, interesting observations about how the cinema influenced the drama (barely two years after the introduction of talkies).

> Dialogue has gradually been growing more natural. It was in-
> evitable that some dramatist should eventually write dialogue
> that exactly copied the average talk, with its hesitations, mum-
> blings and repetitions, and broken sentences, of average people.
> I do not suppose anyone can ever do this with more brilliant ac-
> curacy than Mr. Coward.

The volume also contains *Easy Virtue* and *Hay Fever*, but pride of place is given to *Bitter Sweet*. Given the august reputation of Maugham, it would be wise not to dismiss *Bitter Sweet*.

The score is unbelievably rich. In addition to "I'll See You Again," it has such Coward favorites as "Zigeuner," "Small Little Café," and "Tokay." It also has a signature piece, "If Love Were All," whose lyrics are generally thought to be autobiographical.

NO GOOD AT LOVE

Cole Lesley, Coward's secretary, companion, and confidant, wrote that it would not be entirely accurate to see these lyrics as confessional. His life was obviously more complicated than that, though Coward conceded to Lesley that he had no knack for love. When it came, he was as helpless as anyone without his gifts. Even those gifts deserted him — when he found himself in love, suddenly he could not even see things humorously.

He titled one of his poems straightforwardly "I Am No Good at Love." In it he writes about difficulties with love and betraying it with "little sins." By little sins he meant acts of uncharacteristic — for him — jealousy. He confided to his diary, "I lie awake jeering at myself and, worst of all, pitying myself. All the gallant lyrics of all the songs I have ever written rise up and mock me. To me, passionate love has always been a tight shoe rubbing blisters on my Achilles heel (Oi, Oi, that's enough of that). I resent it and love it and wallow . . . and I wish to God I could handle it but I never have and I know I never will."

Love for Coward meant homosexual love, but that was by no means the source of his insecurities. He accepted it even if society had not made huge advances in understanding or accepting it since the trial of Oscar Wilde in 1895. Nothing about his homosexuality fazed Coward, but he felt no need to declare his orientation or in any way to flaunt it. In 1929, he wrote *Semi-Monde*, a play about young gay men — but it was neither performed nor published. Only late in life, in *A Song at Twilight* (one of three plays collectively titled *Suite in Three Keys*) did he in any way allude to it publicly.

In 1926, he bought himself a Rolls-Royce. By 1930, he was earning 50,000 pounds a year, making him one of the world's highest paid entertainers. Life was not entirely benevolent. In 1927, understandably, given how he had exerted himself, he suffered a nervous breakdown, from which he recovered during a long stay in Hawaii. While there, he wrote another of his most enduring songs, "Room with a View," which made it easier to return to London. Shortly afterward, he also had two massive flops, *Home Chat* and *Sirocco*, both happily long forgotten.

Having achieved such extraordinary success and then experienced these setbacks, he might have been forgiven a withdrawal from his very public life. But Coward had no intention of retreating.

PRIVATE LIVES

Although they were often separated by the Atlantic Ocean — she was often singing his songs on Broadway — Coward and Gertrude Lawrence remained extremely close. He had great admiration for her and promised he would write something expressly for her. Originally that "something" was going to be *Bitter Sweet*, but as he began working on the score, he saw that he was writing material that would strain her vocal limitations. The role was eventually debuted by the American actress Peggy Wood.

In the summer of 1929, Coward was at the Imperial Hotel in Tokyo waiting for his traveling companion, Jeffery Amherst, the same young man who had earlier lured him to New York. He went to bed early in anticipation of Amherst's arrival at seven the next morning. "But the moment I switched out the lights, Gertie appeared in a white Molyneux dress on a terrace in the South of France and refused to go again until four a.m., by which time 'Private Lives,' title and all, had constructed itself."

A few years earlier, he would have spent the next four days writing it. By now, he enjoyed enough success to take a little time to let it percolate. A few weeks later, he was in Shanghai, confined to bed with influenza. Despite his illness, he took out a pencil and began working. Four days later, the play was finished.

He sent it to Lawrence, who, oddly, declared that there was nothing wrong with it that couldn't be fixed. Coward responded to her tepid comment by noting that what would be fixed would be her performance. Onstage it was a triumph for both of them and remains, at least in New York, Coward's most frequently revived play.

It has come to be thought of as a play for a celebrated actress; in the last few decades, it is the female stars who tend to be remembered — Tammy Grimes, Maggie Smith, Lindsay Duncan, and, in darker hours, Joan Collins and Elizabeth Taylor. But both the leading roles must be done by accomplished performers, since, ultimately, there's not a whole lot actually happening.

The curtain rises on two adjoining balconies of a seaside hotel in France. On one, we see Elyot Chase, who is honeymooning with his somewhat younger wife Sybil. On the other, is Amanda Prynne, who is honeymooning with her somewhat staid husband Victor. As it happens, until five years ago Elyot and Amanda were married to one another. The discovery that they are both on their honeymoons astonishes them.

Elyot and Amanda run off with each other to Paris, where Amanda has an apartment. Their spouses catch up with them, but ultimately it is clear that, for all their antagonisms, Elyot and Amanda belong to one another.

When the play was published in 1933, Coward acknowledged that "as a complete play, it leaves a lot to be desired, principally owing to my dastardly and conscienceless behaviour towards Sibyl and Victor, the secondary characters. These, poor things, are little better than ninepins, lightly wooden, and only there at all in order to be repeatedly knocked down . . ."

Earlier he noted that the initial reviews described it as "'tenuous,' 'thin,' 'brittle,' 'gossamer,' 'iridescent,' and delightfully daring.' All of which connoted, to the public mind, 'cocktails,' 'evening dress,' 'repartee,' and irreverent allusions to copulation, thereby causing a gratifying number of respectable people to queue up at the box office."

Like *Hay Fever*, it also has a certain kind of verbal drollery that is unmistakably Coward's.

The world of *Private Lives*, like that of *Hay Fever*, has two classes — the very clever and sophisticated and the ordinary, toward whom the former condescend. By all rights we in the audience should be put off by the condescension of Elyot and Amanda toward their hapless spouses, just as we should be repelled by the airs of superiority of Judith and her family in *Hay Fever*. Part of the odd alchemy of both plays is that we somehow feel the right to identify with the elitists, which is perhaps why we never tire of them.

Early in the play, before the discovery that Elyot is in the room next door, Amanda observes to Victor that doing something remarkable requires a special combination of circumstances — various "thingummys" must come together at the same moment to strike the right spark. "Thingummys" seems a very un-Coward-like word. It suggests Coward acknowledging not everything can be pinned down by his customary verbal precision. The plays celebrate what happens when the spark is struck. It is that moment of the unaccountable that allows us to feel a brief kinship with the Elyots and Amandas and makes these plays, when well performed, endlessly entertaining.

GERTIE

As his earlier comments attest, Coward was not concerned about the literary merits of what he did. He was a performer writing for other entertainers. In Gertrude Lawrence, he found his match.

The same was true of the Lunts. The three had met and hit it off during Coward's first, relatively uneventful visit to New York in 1921. They had wanted him to write a play for all three of them ever since. In 1933, they were all available, and Coward dashed off *Design for Living*.

Like *Hay Fever* and *Private Lives*, *Design* is a soufflé, but it has spent far too much time in the oven. It is overwrought. There are grand speeches for all the major characters. There are surprises galore. First Gilda is sleeping with Leo, the successful playwright. Then Gilda is sleeping with Otto, the successful artist.

Ultimately, she marries Ernest, the successful art dealer — obviously a comedown for her since he has no artistic pretensions. The marriage frees Leo and Otto to declare their love for one another. But ultimately, they return to Gilda and free her from Ernest. The three will now form a ménage a trois, clearly the only solution to their free-floating lusts. The complicated plot and the inevitable but forced conclusion are all heavy-handed. Doubtless with Coward and the Lunts performing it, it had a luster we can only imagine.

The play seems his most "modern," precisely because all the characters are such relentless narcissists. We think of this condition as very now. It has always existed but perhaps has never been so prevalent. To be truly now, though, the character of Ernest would have to be a total narcissist as well — but he lives up to his name and is scandalized by his erstwhile friends. We may side with the elitists as we do in the earlier plays, but they're too serious, too self-dramatizing to provide us much pleasure in their company.

Design for Living was presented in New York in 1932, where it caused an understandable sensation. It could not be done in London until 1939, when mores had changed sufficiently that it did not meet with disfavor from the Lord Chamberlain. (Interestingly, Coward had to do his "command performance" for the censor even to permit performances of *Private Lives*, which strikes us as entirely innocent — its shocks of the tongue-in-cheek variety. Coward was able to persuade the Lord Chamberlain that the second act, in which the formerly married are living together, might be edifying with proper direction and acting.)

ANOTHER SIDE OF NOËL

Only a few months before the opening of *Design for Living*, Coward's most abrasive play (though he would continue writing for another thirty years), London saw a Coward work that revealed a whole new side. Coward had come across a nostalgic photo in a magazine of a troopship carrying British soldiers to the Boer War at the turn of the century. Only a few months earlier, he had briefly played one of the soldiers in the trenches in World War I in R. C. Sherriff's *Journey's End*. He was rehearsing for the London premiere of *Private Lives*, but the photograph and possibly the impressions he gathered working on Sherriff's grim play made him want to try a whole new genre — an epic.

Cavalcade can only be described as an extravaganza. It follows the course of an upper-middle-class family and their servants from the turn of the century until the financial catastrophe of the early '30s. It depicts, among other things, the funeral of Queen Victoria, the *Titanic*, and World War I and ends with a montage of the London of the Bright Young Things — loud, amoral, and chaotic.

At times, it is extremely understated, as when the little son of the cook asks why the queen died. His mother tells him that the queen was very old and very tired, and then asks if he would like another piece of cake.

A love scene takes place on a ship. At the end of the scene, the woman lifts her cloak, which has been hanging over the rail. The cloak has been covering a life belt with the words S.S. *Titanic*. The stage blacks out, and the orchestra plays "very softly and tragically" the hymn it played that fateful night, "Nearer, My God, to Thee." In its conjunction of the intimate and the historic, it is sweepingly panoramic.

The most natural way to describe *Cavalcade* would be cinematic. Coward was acquainted with cinematic epic: He had been an extra in D. W. Griffith's *Hearts of the World*, a propaganda film made in England. Strangely, Coward did not conceive *Cavalcade* for the screen. Its use of crowd scenes and complicated scenery suggests everything would have been easier before the camera than on the stage. On opening night, in fact, one of the two huge stage elevators, filled with an enormous number of extras, stalled for four and a half minutes — to those backstage it seemed like four and a half hours.

Apart from its epic size, what seems surprising, given Coward's output until this time, is its deep, sincere patriotism. The final tableau of mad young London frittering its energies away is succeeded by a spotlight on a huge Union Jack. The chorus, until then singing the cynical "Twentieth Century Blues," now chants "God Save the King."

On October 28, 1931, two weeks after the play opened, King George V and Queen Mary attended a performance. During the second intermission, Coward was presented to them. At the end, the entire audience joined the cast in singing "God Save the King."

Writing about that night years later, Coward observed, "The Queen drew back a little, leaving His Majesty in the front of the box to take the ovation alone. He stood there bowing, looking a little tired, and epitomizing that quality which English people have always deeply valued: unassailable dignity."

It was an important moment in the linking of the country's most popular playwright with its history.

In 1939, at the same time he wrote one of his most glittering dressing-gown plays, *Present Laughter*, Coward wrote a companion piece to *Cavalcade* — *This Happy Breed*. It is about a middle-class family in a neighborhood in South London like the one in which he grew up. *This Happy Breed* begins in 1918 and ends two decades later, as "the clever hopes of a low, dishonest decade" did indeed expire.

It is a remarkably unsentimental look at a middle-class world Coward had not known since he was a child. In some ways, it is a more impressive act of imagination than his upper-class diversions.

Although the overall mood is sympathetically suburban, there is a bit of wit toward the end. Ever the optimist, Aunt Sylvia, a spinster and a pacifist who lives with her brother and his family, declares that Mr. Chamberlain must be a Christian Scientist at heart. Her exasperated niece replies that hopefully Hitler and Mussolini are too — for then no one will have anything to worry about. This exchange takes place in the summer of 1938.

Coward was rehearsing *This Happy Breed* in tandem with *Present Laughter* in late August 1938. With the beginning of the war days later, he withdrew both from production and they did not see the stage until 1942.

"WE MUST HAVE MUSIC"

As ever, alongside his plays, Coward continued to produce the music that kept him in the public eye and heart, regardless of the controversy occasionally produced by the dramas.

"Mad Dogs and Englishman," which he had written two years earlier, was included in a 1932 revue called *Words and Music*, which also contained "Mad About the Boy" and "The Party's over Now." As incidental music for the 1930 *Private Lives*, he wrote "Someday I'll Find You," which was reprised so often during the first act that, at one point, Elyot says acidly, "That orchestra has a remarkably small repertoire."

Even *Cavalcade* had two Coward perennials: "Twentieth Century Blues" and "Lover of My Dreams." (The latter was also reprised endlessly during the four-and-a-half-minute stage-elevator glitch. Coward claimed every time he heard it, it brought back the agony of that wait.)

In 1934, he wrote an operetta, *Conversation Piece*, for the great French light-comedy actress Yvonne Printemps. For many years, he refused to allow it to be performed because he felt it was so much her piece. It contained "I'll Follow My Secret Heart" and the comic "There's Always Something Fishy About the French." It was set in Regency England, a time of unruly anarchy reflected in the boisterous "Regency Rakes."

In 1935, he wrote a set of nine one-acts, collectively called *Tonight at 8:30*, to be performed on successive evenings. The evenings were by no means musicals or revues, but they contained songs. *Red Peppers*, for example, is about a feuding vaudeville couple, perfect parts for Coward and Lawrence. The sketch contains two parodies of genre music of the period, "Has Anybody Seen Our Ship?" and "Men About Town." For some of the other one-acts, he composed two standards, "We Were Dancing" and "Play, Orchestra, Play."

In 1937, he wrote another operetta in the style of *Bitter Sweet*, this one called *Operette*. Several songs were written expressly for a Viennese singer named Fritzi Massary, who enchanted everyone who remembered her. The great British comic actor George Rose extolled her talents.

The celebrated agent Robbie Lantz had known Massary back in Vienna and remained in touch with her when she moved to Los

Angeles, where she ended her days. He had praised her so extravagantly to his client Mike Nichols that Nichols begged to be introduced to her. As they left her house, Nichols turned to Lantz and said, "You barely did her justice." It was for her that Coward, clearly also taken with her charms, wrote the title song of *Operette*.

ACTORS AND WRITERS

Over the years, Coward had maintained excellent relationships with the actors who appeared in his plays, not an easy thing considering that he was unquestionably the star and made sure that he had more than his share of the best moments. Nevertheless, his eye for talent and capacity for friendship were admirable.

For *The Vortex*, with which he had made such a splash near the beginning of his West End career, he chose as his understudy a fledgling actor named John Gielgud, who replaced him after he left the cast. Three decades later, in the 1956 *Nude with Violin*, a play in which he did not appear, he created a leading role for Gielgud.

He readily acknowledged that the roles of Victor and Sibyl in *Private Lives* were indeed secondary. But he did not cast them with secondary actors. The role of Victor was originally played by an extremely talented young actor named Laurence Olivier, for whom it was the jump-start to a towering career. (Sybil was played by Adrianne Allen, with whom Coward maintained a lifelong friendship.)

During the 1930s, his writing was often geared toward specific actors. As we have seen, *Conversation Piece* was entirely conceived for Yvonne Printemps. *Operette* was written with Fritzi Massary in mind as well as Peggy Wood, the American actress who created the lead in *Bitter Sweet*.

Similarly, the plays he wrote in the '30s were tailored toward talents he understood. Several of the nine one-acts of *Tonight at 8:30* were written to give him another chance to act with Lawrence. *Red Peppers*, with the battling vaudeville couple, was a perfect vehicle for their gifts of banter musical.

The best known of these one-acts, of course, is *Still Life*, which is about the love affair of two quite ordinary people, both of whom happen to be married to other people. They meet over a period of time in the buffet of a rural railroad station. There is no more perfect expression of the British ability to both experience and repress deep emotion. Coward rewrote it during the war, and it was filmed as *Brief Encounter.*

It was no small matter that he had an accurate sense of his own talent. *Fumed Oak* was a remarkable change of pace. He played Henry Gow, the father of an unhappy lower-middle-class family. He and his wife live with her sharp-tongued mother and their enervating, abrasive daughter. The play culminates in Gow denouncing them in frustration, a far cry from the world of the Bright Young Things.

Coward's last foray into that charmed world was *Present Laughter*, in which he created for himself the role of the matinee idol Garry Essendine, a wildly successful, egotistical man separated from his wife and enjoying the company of many other women. In one scene, he is assaulted by a beautiful woman in whom he has no interest.

In addition to the vintage brittle dialogue, there is an interesting exchange between Essendine and a humorless young playwright who bursts into his fashionable, luxurious world. He can indeed be considered an "angry young man," a decade and a half before that became the fashion for British playwrights. Essendine tells him his play is a meaningless jumble that bears no relation to the theater or life or anything. It is hard to know what precipitated the outburst. *Present Laughter* is about seduction and the vanities of the leisure class. When it was written, that was exactly what the audiences expected an evening in the theater to be.

Critics, however, were changing course. Cyril Connolly, then one of the most formidable figures of English literary life, reviewed Coward's first memoir, *Present Indicative*, on its publication in 1937.

He called Coward "one of the most talented and prodigiously success-ful people the world has ever known — a person of infinite charm and adaptability whose very adaptability however makes him inferior to a more compact and worldly competitor in his own sphere, like Cole Porter; and an essentially unhappy man, a man who gives one the impression of having seldom really thought or really lived and who is intelligent enough to know it. . . . There is only success, more and more of it . . . and that even is temporary. For one can't read any of Noël Coward's plays now . . . they are written in the most topical and perishable way imaginable, the cream in them turns sour overnight — they are even dead before they are turned into talkies, however engag-ing they may seem at the time . . ."

But from wherever on Mount Olympus Connolly was perched, few literary reputations seemed substantial. Of Virginia Woolf, he con-fided to his journal, "She is not really a novelist. . . . she does not care for human beings. . . . Her critical essays are riddled with clichés."

The world in which Connolly passed such ultra-fastidious judg-ments and Coward enjoyed such apparently unmerited success was about to change irrevocably.

THE WAR YEARS

With the commencement of the war in September 1939, Coward found himself spending a lot of time in Paris. Along with the French playwright Jean Giraudoux, he was organizing an office of wartime propaganda. The Germans, it was assumed, would be kept at bay by the Maginot Line, but there was concern for the morale of the French under siege. Interestingly, both the British and French governments thought these matters would best be served by a leading playwright.

The suddenness with which the Germans overran France in the spring of 1940 was a great surprise. Coward, who was in America at the time, wanted to return to France to close the office and make sure there were no papers of importance the Germans might come upon. He was forbidden to do so. After the war, he discovered his name on a list of English notables the Nazis wanted captured and killed. Among them was Rebecca West, who wrote him a postcard observing, "Just think of the people we'd have been seen dead with!" When he went back to Paris after the war, he discovered that his loyal maid had taken all his papers and sealed them inside a wall of her apartment.

Coward had hoped he might be able to do intelligence work, but the new prime minister, his longtime friend Winston Churchill, thought he could do nothing more important than sing "Mad Dogs and Englishmen" and his other songs to the troops. Reluctantly, he agreed, performing in America, Australia, the Middle East, Africa, and India. To his surprise and that of many others, the troops responded enthusiastically to this somewhat aristocratic figure with perfect, clipped diction.

There was an awkward moment when he was due to perform before some American soldiers. He had caused a scandal in the publication of a wartime memoir in which he belittled some Brooklyn soldiers he described as "sniveling" over relatively minor wounds. The remark was seen as anti-Semitic. Mayor Fiorello LaGuardia created an organization to prevent "the Bum" from ever returning to America. Beatrice Lillie, who was in New York at the time, made a contribution to the organization in Coward's name and sent him his membership card.

How, a friend wondered, would he handle an appearance in newly liberated Paris before an audience composed largely of Americans? On that occasion, his entrance, usually greeted by wild applause, was met with deadly silence. After a pause, he addressed them, "Ladies and gentlemen and all you dear, dear sniveling little boys from Brooklyn." It produced a roar of laughter. The audience was with him.

His major contribution to the war effort was a film he wrote with the help of his longtime friend Lord Mountbatten, *In Which We Serve*, a tribute to the Royal Navy in the style of *Cavalcade*. To his astonishment, the wartime censors almost did not give permission for the film to be made.

Based on an actual incident in which Mountbatten had been involved, it depicted the sinking of a ship, which the bureaucrats thought might not be good for morale. Coward pointed out that in wartime quite a lot of ships were sunk and that what the film was about was the bravery of the men on them.

The censor acquiesced. *In Which We Serve* won a special Oscar the year it was released and remains an extremely moving tribute to the British spirit.

In 1943, he wrote a song satirizing the attitude of a lot of "peace-loving" Brits who advocated clemency toward the Nazis when the war ended. It was called "Don't Let's Be Beastly to the Germans." When he sang it at a private party, Winston Churchill, laughing heartily, asked him to reprise it three times. But when, shortly afterward, he sang it on the BBC, it created an uproar. Many listeners could not see the thinly veiled irony of lines like, "Let's help the dirty swine again / To occupy the Rhine again."

A source of some antipathy at the beginning of the war was the amount of time he was spending in Paris. His propaganda activities were a secret, but to the meddlesome Fleet Street Paris, he seemed to be enjoying himself at a time of crisis. British intelligence also sent him to America in the years when most Americans thought the war was taking place "over there" and would not involve them. He raised money for a British orphanage he had adopted and also tried to raise Americans' consciousness about the true stakes of what was happening "over there."

While he was engaged in this work, parliament enacted a currency law that made it an offense to have more than a certain number of pounds sterling abroad. On his return, he was indicted under this law, though much of the currency he had went to subsidize shows he produced to raise money for British charities. He was entirely cooperative and was punished with minor fines.

His friend, King George VI, wanted to knight him for his wartime services but another of his friends, Winston Churchill, thought this would be inadvisable after the currency affair.

He ought to have received a knighthood simply for the song "London Pride," which he wrote one morning after a severe bombing by the Germans. What impressed him was the resoluteness of his fellow Londoners going about their tasks as if what had happened were normal. (Perhaps it was the lack of that stiff upper lip that had irritated him about the wounded Americans.)

Even before the war ended, the Brits held elections and threw Churchill out of power, which disgusted Coward on many levels. He shared the sense of triumph the British had in winning the war but found himself less and less at home in the country whose spirit he had once so vividly embodied. He found himself eager to spend more time elsewhere.

Goldenhurst, his country estate, had been requisitioned by the army during the war. It had undergone considerable damage, and given severe post-war rationing, it would take a long time to be restored. During the war, he had bought a house in Jamaica, where he spent more and more time. In the 1950s, he also acquired a house in Switzerland, where one of his neighbors was the great Australian soprano Joan Sutherland, who made an album of his songs in 1966.

BACK TO WRITING

An unalloyed triumph he had achieved during the war was the success of *Blithe Spirit*, which enjoyed a run longer than any of his earlier successes. Unlike most of his previous major works, it had no part for him, which gave all its characters a greater equality. Although it remains one of his most popular works and is thought to be "typical" Noël Coward, it is worlds away from the plays that created his initial reputation.

The play is set in the country house of a novelist, Charles

Condomine, who has been investigating the occult for his new book. He hires a local medium, the dizzy Madame Arcati, to conduct a séance. In doing so, she summons up the ghost of the writer's late wife, Elvira, who died seven years earlier and who cannot conceal her antipathy for Ruth, the woman who has succeeded her.

Elvira botches her attempt to kill Condomine in a car accident, instead killing Ruth. Ruth's ghost immediately returns to the house, seeking revenge on Elvira. Madame Arcati not being the most expert of mediums, her attempts to resolve the situation only make matters worse. At the end, she advises Condomine to quit his house as the ghosts of both ex-wives wreak havoc in its hitherto genteel interior.

The play ran in the West End for 1,777 performances, a record for a nonmusical. The role of Madame Arcati has been a plum for aging actresses. Margaret Rutherford debuted the role and also played Arcati in the post-war film version that starred Rex Harrison. In the United States, the role was first played by Mildred Natwick, who also did it in a TV version in the '50s. In 2009, a revival featured Angela Lansbury as the medium, for which she won a Tony.

In 1964, a musical version, with score by Hugh Martin and Timothy Gray, not Coward, opened on Broadway with Beatrice Lillie as Madame Arcati. In the chorus was a young dancer named Christopher Walken, who recalled years later that the dancers always waited to hear her do a song with her Ouija board. They always timed the applause she received. One night it lasted fully six minutes.

Few of Coward's post-war plays enjoyed such renown. In 1947, *Peace in Our Time*, originally titled *What Might Have Been*, was produced in the West End. It was a very uncharacteristic work — an imagining of what Britain might have been like if it had been invaded by Germany, as France had been. Despite mixed-to-favorable notices, it did not find an audience, perhaps because the war was still making people's lives difficult, and no one wanted to spend an evening dwelling on the unhappiness of those years, even if the misfortunes had been re-imagined and transformed.

Interestingly, with the exception of *Relative Values*, which is about a titled family whose heir wants to marry a Hollywood actress — hardly the most startling of themes — many of the post-war plays seem exercises in nostalgia. Just after the war, for example, he wrote another operetta, *Pacific 1860*, as a vehicle for Mary Martin.

It was a love story set in nineteenth-century Jamaica. The rehearsal period was one of sustained tension between star and writer, aggravated by the star's husband, Richard Halliday, who acted as her manager and spokesperson. That it was a flop did not improve their relationship, and they were only reconciled years later, when Martin had become celebrated for her role in *South Pacific*. Coward had mixed feelings about the show, perhaps because he sensed how old-fashioned it made many of his musical efforts seem.

For the Lunts, he wrote *Quadrille*, a play set in the Victorian era. It was, of course, another triumph for them, but it has almost never been revived because without the intangibles of their performances, the play has little vitality of its own.

In 1953, Coward wrote a musical version of Oscar Wilde's *Lady Windermere's Fan* called *After the Ball*. Robert Helpmann, who directed *After the Ball*, analyzed its weaknesses with some surprise: "You would have thought that a play of Wilde's with music by Noël Coward should be marvelous, but I suddenly realized at the first rehearsal it was like having two funny people at a dinner party. Everything that Coward sent up Wilde was sentimental about, and everything that Wilde sent up Coward was sentimental about. It was two different points of view and it didn't work. It could never have worked."

He began writing *Nude with Violin* for himself but then rewrote it for John Gielgud, who enjoyed a modest success on Broadway with it, where it opened in 1957. He played a butler who has served an artist faithfully for many years. At the end of the play, he has a marvelous scene reading the artist's bitter, caustic will to the exceedingly unhappy heirs. The play exuded an antipathy toward contemporary art that would soon reveal itself in other ways.

Coward followed *Nude with Violin* with *Look After Lulu!*, a translation of the nineteenth-century Feydeaux farce *Occupe-toi d'Amelie*. It flopped, despite having Vivien Leigh in the starring role.

NEW MEDIA

If Coward did not distinguish himself with his dramatic writing during the '50s, he found other avenues to explore. He worked more as an actor, performing in Shaw's *The Devil's Disciple* in the West End and in movies like his friend Graham Greene's *Our Man in Havana*.

Television, which was then still geared toward the upper-middle-class audiences that could, in the early days, afford to have the rather grandiose pieces of furniture that passed for TV sets, was extremely receptive to his work. One of his lesser-known plays, *This Happy Breed*, was a great success on both sides of the Atlantic. *Blithe Spirit* was an understandable triumph.

Having been reconciled with Mary Martin and her difficult husband, he agreed to do a ninety-minute special for American television, *Together with Music*. Though he did not generally take to criticism of his writing, he thought their comments on the first version were valid and rewrote it. Much of it consisted of the two of them singing standards, many of them Coward's own. It was extremely well received.

Perhaps his most astonishing new venture was into the world of cabaret. He made his nightclub debut at the Café de Paris in London in 1954. In some ways, his success was not surprising. Many in the audience must have been present for his early theater successes when they — and he — were young. Now both were well-heeled and more comfortable in gilded nightclubs than the increasingly "kitchen-sink-oriented" theaters.

What was, perhaps, more surprising was his agreement to appear at the Desert Inn in Las Vegas, hardly a place that seemed a natural for him. But the offer was $40,000 a week, which he needed to pay back taxes in an England that levied crippling taxes on the wealthy to support its fledgling socialist experiments. (For this reason, Coward spent minimal time there, spending far more time in Jamaica.)

His Las Vegas engagement turned out to be yet another success, luring his glamorous friends from both coasts there. Whether the inveterate gamblers dropped in on his shows is a question, but he helped give Las Vegas a kind of glamour that was not part of its traditional image.

YOUNGER ANGER

In 1955 John Osborne's *Look Back in Anger* opened at the Royal Court Theater in London. Osborne's tirade against post-war Britain became a sensation. Olivier went and made his irritation known, which created a public stir — leading eventually to his making the gesture of asking Osborne to write something for him. That something turned out to be *The Entertainer*, a milestone for both of them.

Coward found *Look Back in Anger* full of vitality. But Osborne's succeeding plays, including *The Entertainer*, made him doubt his original assessment of Osborne's talent.

Coward's first exposure to the work of Harold Pinter was a double bill of *The Dumbwaiter* and *The Room* at the Royal Court. "They were completely incomprehensible and insultingly boring, although fairly well acted. It is the surrealist school of non-playwriting." He was pleased to see that though they had received good reviews, "Nobody was there."

A few months later, however, when he saw *The Caretaker*, he had a sense of the originality of Pinter's talent. "On the face of it, [it] is everything I hate most in the theater — squalor, repetition, lack of action, etc. — but somehow it seizes hold of you," he wrote in his diary. He added that he wished he could see the earlier plays again because he now might appreciate them more. "He is at least a genuine original. I don't think he could write in any other way if he tried."

In a series of articles for the *Sunday Times* in 1961, Coward declared his lack of interest in the angry young men. "I am quite prepared to admit that during my fifty-odd years of theatergoing, I have on many occasions been profoundly moved by plays about the Common Man, as in my fifty-odd years of restaurant-going I have enjoyed tripe and onions, but I am not prepared to admit that an exclusive diet of either would be completely satisfying."

Kenneth Tynan, who championed the younger writers, responded that, "The bridge of a sinking ship . . . is scarcely the ideal place to deliver a lecture on the technique of keeping afloat."

In 1966, Osborne wrote Coward a letter praising *Suite in Three Keys*, in which he wrote, "Now: I would like to ask a favor of you. Could you, in future, stop assessing your fellow writers to newspaper reporters? Clearly it gives them pleasure but you scarcely need their approval. I have always had the profoundest respect for you, both for what you do and as a unique and moving figure on our landscape."

All these antagonists eventually became good friends. Pinter even invited him to watch the filming of *The Homecoming*, a play for which Coward had particular admiration. He accepted the invitation. Years later, Pinter directed a revival of *Blithe Spirit* at the National Theatre.

LATER YEARS

Writing and acting were so much in his blood that, even as the years wore on, he continued to do both. In the early '60s, he wrote two musicals expressly for Broadway. *Sail Away*, which took its title from one of Coward's most personal songs that he had written a decade earlier, was a satire on life aboard an ocean liner. The 1961 show was originally to have starred Kay Thompson, whom Coward had known for many years. She was both an expert musician and a droll comedienne, but she withdrew before rehearsals began and was replaced by Elaine Stritch.

A member of the chorus recalled that when the show tried out in Boston, it was in reasonably good shape, but Coward kept rewriting it to make it a star vehicle for Stritch. These efforts did not help the show as a whole, though they provided Stritch with cabaret material for many years to come.

In 1963, he agreed to turn Terence Rattigan's *The Sleeping Prince* into a musical, which was titled *The Girl Who Came to Supper*. Rattigan's play had been made into a movie starring Olivier and Marilyn Monroe, which made it a well-known property. The musical, for which Coward composed a long tribute to the English music-hall tradition, felt strained.

The two works that show how extraordinarily sound his theatrical instincts remained were the 1960 *Waiting in the Wings*, a comedy about women in a British home for retired actors, and the 1966 *Suite in Three Keys*, three one-acts set in different times in a hotel suite in Switzerland. *Wings* is indeed a comedy but in ways not common in Coward's oeuvre. Its banter concealed a lot of pathos, which is understandable in a work in which the verb *waiting* has very dark meanings.

The most interesting of the three plays in *Suite* is *A Song at Twilight*, in which an aging author modeled on Somerset Maugham, whom Coward had come to dislike, agrees to meet with an old lover. She brings him some love letters she has held in the many years since they were together, letters that make clear he had had a male lover in his youth. It was the only time Coward alluded to the subject of homosexuality in his works, and though the play has the same discretion that Coward regarded as essential in his life, the allusion struck many as interesting.

RENAISSANCE

His skirmishes with the Angry Young Men, though they elicited great support from the older generation of theatergoers, did not endear him to the young audiences who identified with Osborne's railing antihero. It would have been easy in the early '60s to see Coward as the representative of a lost world, a world that, given its shallow values, was indeed well lost.

In 1964, Olivier was the artistic director of Britain's National Theatre, which specialized in peerless productions of Britain's classics, especially Shakespeare. Olivier decided it was time for the National to revive the work of a living English playwright. He decided to present *Hay Fever* and invited Coward to direct it. The production, which starred Edith Evans and Maggie Smith, reminded theatergoers of the sheer unalloyed pleasure to be found in Coward's comedies.

From then on, the only proper attitude toward Coward was celebration. A new spate of revivals, including one of *Private Lives* starring Maggie Smith, reminded the public of just how expertly these plays had been fashioned. His film-acting career continued. He played opposite Michael Caine as a criminal mastermind in *The Italian Job*. Caine said it was "a bit like playing with God," only one manifestation of the huge reservoirs of affection in which he was held. With Olivier, he appeared in an Otto Preminger film, *Bunny Lake Is Missing*. He appeared alongside Richard Burton and Elizabeth Taylor in *Boom*, a film version of Tennessee Williams' *The Milk Train Doesn't Stop Here Any More*.

In New York there was a revue of his music called *Oh, Coward*. A similar revue in London was called *Cowardy Custard*. Both reminded the public of the wealth of his music.

In 1969 for his seventieth birthday, the BBC presented his movies and TV and radio plays, including *In Which We Serve*, which had only become more moving over the years. Coward himself referred to the celebration as "Holy Week."

The high point was a birthday luncheon hosted by Queen Elizabeth II, whom he had known and whose company he had enjoyed since she was a girl. It was attended by members of the nobility and members of Britain's theatrical nobility. Obeying proper etiquette, she asked him if he would accept a knighthood. For once, the wittiest man in England could make no smart reply. He was, in fact, moved.

The following spring in New York, he was given a special Tony Award. The ceremony was attended by his friends, Alfred Lunt and

Lynn Fontanne, and another Englishman who had made good in America, Cary Grant.

Coward died March 26, 1973, in his bed in Jamaica. The outpouring of grief and love belied the conventional notions of British reserve.

In the cast of *Song at Twilight* had been his old friend Irene Worth. On opening night, she wrote him a letter thanking him for all he had done in his long, fabulous career. She cited a line from the play "which has struck me so deeply and meant so much to me that I must thank you — from my heart — for such a profound and precious lesson which I shall never forget — 'Life — our most important responsibility.'"

When Coward first understood the magnitude of his talent is hard to know, but he never ceased to serve it. The fulfillment of his talent complemented his unfailing gift for friendship. Both were evidence of his understanding of his responsibility to life.

SUGGESTED EXCERPTS

from the Major Plays

IN AN HOUR BOOKS, LLC regrets the absence, in this volume, of representative excerpts from the plays of Noël Coward. We were denied permission by Random House Publishers, who control the rights. The reason given was that Random House intends to publish a book about Noël Coward in 2011 and doesn't want competition from our book.

We respectfully submit that in this instance, the permissions policy of Random House does not reflect the intention of the copyright law to protect the public's interest in the copyrighted intellectual property represented by the plays of Noël Coward but rather extends the protection of the copyright holder's interest in the property beyond what the copyright law intends to grant.

It is our view that copyright use policies such as this will serve the interests of those who are working to diminish and eventually to eliminate copyright protection for creators of intellectual property.

A guide to accessing the selected excerpts follows.

These excerpt suggestions are from the playwright's major plays. They are meant to give a taste of the playwright's work. The suggested excerpts, which are in chronological order, illustrate the main themes mentioned in the In an Hour essay. Premiere dates are provided.

from **Private Lives** (1930)
Act One

CHARACTERS

Elyot
Amanda
Victor
Sibyl

In the middle of Act One Amanda and Elyot, once married, now honeymooning with new spouses in adjoining hotel rooms, reminisce about their tumultuous marriage in the scene that begins with Elyot's line, "We were so ridiculously in love."

from **Design for Living** (1932)
Act One

CHARACTERS

Leo

Gilda

In the middle of Act One, Gilda and Leo, who have been in and out of love with each other as well as their mutual friend Otto, dissect their complex relationship in the scene that begins with Leo's line, "Can't we put an end to this flagellation party now?"

from **Still Life***, from* **Tonight at 8:30** (1936)
Scene 2 from this one-act play

CHARACTERS

Alec
Laura
Ticket Inspector
Albert

Alec, a doctor, and Laura, a housewife, have met by chance in the refreshment room of a provincial railroad station. Both married, they begin an affair. In Scene 2 of this one-act play, Alec tries to reassure Laura in the dialogue that begins, "We haven't done anything wrong."

from **Blithe Spirit** (1941)
from Act One

CHARACTERS

Ruth
Charles
Elvira

In the middle of Act One, Charles, whose late first wife Elvira has been conjured up by a medium, tries to make his current wife, Ruth, understand that Elvira's mischievous ghost is in the room. The scene begins with Ruth's line, "Would you say the evening has been profitable?"

CHARACTERS

Hugo
Charlotta

In the middle of Act One, Scene 2, Hugo, a successful writer who is
bisexual, confronts his former wife, Carlotta, who has letters he wrote
to a male lover. The scene begins with Hugo's line, "I am finding the
flippancy of your manner extremely irritating."

THE READING ROOM

YOUNG ACTORS AND THEIR TEACHERS

Hoare, Philip. *Noël Coward: A Biography.* London: Sinclair-Stevenson 1995.

SCHOLARS, STUDENTS, PROFESSORS

Castle, Charles. *Noël.* London: W. H. Allen, 1972.

Guthrie, Tyrone. *A Life in the Theatre.* London: Hamish Hamilton, 1960.

Lahr, John. *Coward the Playwright.* Berkeley: University of California Press, 2002

Lesley, Cole. *The Life of Noël Coward.* London: Jonathan Cape, 1976.

_____. *Remembered Laughter.* New York: Knopf, 1978.

Lesley, Cole, Sheridan Morley, and Graham Payn. *Noel Coward and his Friends.* New York: Morrow, 1979.

Morley, Sheridan. *Gertrude Lawrence.* New York: McGraw-Hill, 1981.

_____. *A Talent to Amuse.* Boston, Little Brown, 1985.

THEATERS, PRODUCERS

Mander, Raymond, and Joe Mitchenson. *Theatrical Companion to Coward.* Updated by Barry Day and Sheridan Morley. London: Oberon Books, 2000.

ACTORS, DIRECTORS, THEATER PROFESSIONALS

Burton, Hal, ed. *Great Acting; Laurence Olivier, Sybil Thorndike, Ralph Richardson, Peggy Ashcroft, Michael Redgrave, Edith Evens, John Geilgud, Noël Coward.* London: British Broadcast Corporation, 1968.

Kaplan, Joel, and Sheila Stowell. *Look Back in Pleasure: Noël Coward Reconsidered.* London: Methuen, 2000.

This extensive bibliography lists books about the playwright according to whom the books might be of interest. If you would like to research further something that interests you in the text, lists of references, sources cited, and editions used in this book are found in this section.

Morley, Sheridan. *A Talent to Amuse*. London: Penguin 1974.

Payn, Graham. *My Life with Noël Coward*. New York: Applause Books, 1994.

Richards, Dick. *The Wit of Noël Coward*. London: Sphere Books, 1970.

EDITIONS OF COWARD'S WORKS USED FOR THIS BOOK

Coward, Noël. *Present Indicative*. Garden City, N.Y.: Doubleday, 1937.

_____. *Future Conditional*. Garden City, N.Y.: Doubleday, 1954.

_____. *A Last Encore*. Edited by John Hadfield. Boston: Little, Brown, 1973.

_____. *Diaries*. Graham Payn and Sheridan Morley. Boston: Little Brown, 1982.

_____. *Collected Verse*. Edited by Graham Payn and Martin Ticknor. London: Methuen, 1984.

_____. *Complete Lyrics*. Edited by Barry Day. New York: Overlook, 1998.

_____. *Collected Plays*. Vols.1–8. Edited by Sheridan Morley. London: Methuen, 1999.

_____. *The Letters of Noel Coward*. Edited by Barry Day. New York: Knopf, 2007.

SOURCES CITED IN THIS BOOK

Coward, Noël. *Bitter Sweet and Other Plays*. Introduction by W. Somerset Maugham. New York: Doubleday Doran, 1929.

_____. *Middle East Diary*. London: The Right Book Club, 1945.

_____. *The Noël Coward Diaries*. Edited by Graham Payn and Sheridan Morley. Introduction by John Lahr. Boston: Little Brown, 1982.

_____. *The Letters of Noël Coward*. Edited by Barry Day. New York: Knopf, 2007.

Lantz, Robbie. Personal reminiscence to the author about Fritzi Massary.

Tynan, Kenneth. *Curtains*. New York: Atheneum, 1961.

Awards

"And the winner is . . . "

NOËL COWARD HONORS AND AWARDS

Cavalcade was awarded two Academy awards for best director and best art direction (play by Noël Coward, screenplay by Reginald Berkeley and Sonya Levien, directed by Frank Lloyd), 1934.

In Which We Serve received an Academy Honorary Award for outstanding achievement (Noël Coward wrote the screenplay, the music, and co-directed the film.), 1943. It also won the 1942 New York Film Critics Circle Award for Best Motion Picture and the 1943 Argentine Film Critics Association Award for Best Foreign Film.

Blithe Spirit was awarded the New York Drama Critics Circle Award for Best Foreign Play, 1942.

He was knighted by Queen Elizabeth II and elected fellow of the Royal Society of Literature.

In 1970 Noël Coward received a special Tony Award for "multiple and immortal contributions to the theater."

	PULITZER PRIZE	TONY AWARD	NY DRAMA CRITICS CIRCLE AWARD		
			Best American	Best Foreign	Best Play
1918	Jesse Lynch Williams *Why Marry?*	-	-		
1919	No Award	-	-		
1920	Eugene O'Neill *Beyond the Horizon*	-	-		
1921	Zona Gale *Miss Lulu Bett*	-	-		
1922	Eugene O'Neill *Anna Christie*	-	-		

This awards chart is provided for reference so you can see who was winning the major writing awards during the writing career of the playwright.

	PULITZER PRIZE	TONY AWARD	NY DRAMA CRITICS CIRCLE AWARD		
			Best American	Best Foreign	Best Play
1923	Owen Davis *Icebound*	-	-		
1924	Hatcher Hughes *Hell-Bent Fer Heaven*	-	-		
1925	Sidney Howard *They Knew What They Wanted*	-	-		
1926	George Kelly *Craig's Wife*	-	-		
1927	Paul Green *In Abraham's Bosom*	-	-		
1928	Eugene O'Neill *Strange Interlude*	-	-		
1929	Elmer L. Rice *Street Scene*	-	-		
1930	Marc Connelly *The Green Pastures*	-	-		
1931	Susan Glaspell *Alison's House*	-	-		
1932	George S. Kaufman *Of Thee I Sing*	-	-		
1933	Maxwell Anderson *Both Your Houses*	-	-		
1934	Sidney Kingsley *Men in White*	-	-		
1935	Zoe Akins *The Old Maid*	-	-		
1936	Robert E. Sherwood *Idiot's Delight*	-	Maxwell Anderson *Winterset*		
1937	Moss Hart and George S. Kaufman *You Can't Take It With You*	-	Maxwell Anderson *High Tor*		
1938	Thornton Wilder *Our Town*	-	John Steinbeck *Of Mice and Men*		
1939	Robert E. Sherwood *Abe Lincoln in Illinois*	-	No Award		
1940	William Saroyan *The Time of Your Life*	-	William Saroyan *The Time of Your Life*		
1941	Robert E. Sherwood *There Shall Be No Night*	-	Lillian Hellman *Watch on the Rhine*		

	PULITZER PRIZE	TONY AWARD	NY DRAMA CRITICS CIRCLE AWARD		
			Best American	Best Foreign	Best Play
1942	No Award	-	No Award		
1943	Thornton Wilder *The Skin of Our Teeth*	-	Sidney Kingsley *The Patriots*		
1944	No Award	-	No Award		
1945	Mary Chase *Harvey*	-	Tennessee Williams *The Glass Managerie*		
1946	Russel Crouse and Howard Lindsay *State of the Union*	-	No Award		
1947	No Award	Arthur Miller *All My Sons*	Arthur Miller *All My Sons*		
1948	Tennessee Williams *A Streetcar Named Desire*	Joshua Logan and Thomas Heggen *Mister Roberts*	Tennessee Williams *A Streetcar Named Desire*		
1949	Arthur Miller *Death of a Salesman*	Arthur Miller *Death of a Salesman*	Arthur Miller *Death of a Salesman*		
1950	Richard Rodgers *South Pacific*	T.S. Eliot *The Cocktail Party*	Carson McCullers *A Member of the Wedding*		
1951	No Award	Tennessee Williams *The Rose Tattoo*	Sidney Kingsley *Darkness at Noon*		
1952	Joseph Kramm *The Shrike*	Jan de Hartog *The Fourposter*	John van Druten *I Am a Camera*		
1953	\William Inge *Picnic*	Arthur Miller *The Crucible*	William Inge *Picnic*		
1954	John Patrick *The Teahouse of the August Moon*	John Patrick *The Teahouse of the August Moon*	John Patrick *The Teahouse of the August Moon*		
1955	Tennessee Williams *Cat on a Hot Tin Roof*	Joseph Hayes *The Desperate Hours*	Tennessee Williams *Cat on a Hot Tin Roof*		
1956	Albert Hackett and Frances Goodrich *The Diary of Anne Frank*	Albert Hackett and Frances Goodrich *The Diary of Anne Frank*	Albert Hackett and Frances Goodrich *The Diary of Anne Frank*		
1957	Eugene O'Neill *Long Days Journey Into Night*	Eugene O'Neill *Long Days Journey Into Night*	Eugene O'Neill *Long Days Journey Into Night*		
1958	Ketti Frings *Look Homeward, Angel*	Dore Schary *Sunrise At Campobello*	Ketti Frings *Look Homeward, Angel*		
1959	Archibald Macleish *J.B.*	Archibald Macleish *J.B.*	Lorraine Hansberry *A Raisin in the Sun*		

	PULITZER PRIZE	TONY AWARD	NY DRAMA CRITICS CIRCLE AWARD		
			Best American	Best Foreign	Best Play
1960	Jerry Bock, music Sheldon Harnick, lyrics Jerome Wiedman, book George Abbott, book *Fiorello!*	William Gibson *The Miracle Worker*	Lillian Hellman *Toys in the Attic*		
1961	Tad Mosel *All the Way Home*	Jean Anouilh *Beckett*	Tad Mosel *All the Way Home*		
1962	Frank Loesser and Abe Burrows *How to Succeed in Business Without Really Trying*	Robert Bolt *A Man for All Seasons*	Tennessee Williams *The Night of the Iguana*	Richard Bolt *A Man for All Seasons*	No Award
1963	No Award	Edward Albee *Who's Afraid of Virginia Woolf?*	Edward Albee *Who's Afraid of Virginia Woolf?*		
1964	No Award	John Osborne *Luther*	John Osborne *Luther*		
1965	Frank D. Gilroy *The Subject Was Roses*	Frank D. Gilroy *The Subject Was Roses*	Frank D. Gilroy *The Subject Was Roses*		
1966	No Award	Peter Weiss *Marat / Sade*	Peter Weiss *Marat / Sade*		
1967	Edward Albee *A Delicate Balance*	Harold Pinter *The Homecoming*	Harold Pinter *The Homecoming*		
1968	No Award	Tom Stoppard *Rosencrantz and Guildenstern Are Dead*	Tom Stoppard *Rosencrantz and Guildenstern Are Dead*		
1969	Howard Sackler *The Great White Hope*	Howard Sackler *The Great White Hope*	Howard Sackler *The Great White Hope*		
1970	Charles Gordone *No Place to Be Somebody*	Frank McMahon *Borstal Boy*	Paul Zindel *The Effect of Gamma Rays on Man-in-the- Moon Marigolds*	No Award	Frank McMahon *Borstal Boy*
1971	Paul Zindel *The Effect of Gamma Rays on Man-in-the- Moon Marigolds*	Anthony Shaffer *Sleuth*	John Guare *The House of Blue Leaves*	No Award	David Storey *Home*
1972	No Award	David Rabe *Sticks and Bones*	No Award	Jean Genet *The Screens*	Jason Miller *That Cham- pionship Season*
1973	Jason Miller *That Championship Season*	Jason Miller *That Champion Season*	Lanford Wilson *The Hot L Baltimore*	No Award	David Storey *The Changing Room*

INDEX

The entries in the index include highlights from the main In an Hour essay portion of the book.